AMAZING SCIENCE

KILLER WHALES

AND OTHER

FROZEN WORLD WONDERS

Q.L. PEARCE
Illustrated by Mary Ann Fraser

Julian Messner

Dedication....

To my mom, with thanks for everything   *—Q.L. Pearce*
To Patsy, Sally, Anita, and Judy   *—Mary Ann Fraser*

Acknowledgments

With thanks to Jill S. Schneiderman, Ph.D., Assistant Professor of
Geology, Pomona College, Claremont, California, for her invaluable
assistance and critical review of the manuscript.

Library of Congress Cataloging-in-Publication Data
Pearce, Q. L. (Querida Lee)
    Killer whales and other frozen world wonders / Q.L. Pearce;
illustrated by Mary Ann Fraser.
        p. cm.—(Amazing science)
    Includes bibliographical references and index.
    Summary: Describes the earth's polar regions and the animals that live
there, including the seal, penguin, musk ox, and polar bear.
    1. Polar regions—Juvenile literature. [1. Polar regions. 2. Zoology—Polar
regions.] I. Fraser, Mary Ann, ill. II. Title. III. Series: Pearce, Q.L. (Querida
Lee). Amazing science.
G590.P43 1991   90-20320
919.8—dc20   CIP

ISBN 0-671-70693-4 (lib. bdg.)
ISBN 0-671-70694-2 (pbk.)

Contents

Frozen Worlds

For centuries, the icy worlds at the ends of the earth—the Arctic in the North and Antarctic in the South—have fired human imaginations. Early Arctic voyagers returned home with stories of islands that vanished and of people made of ice. Until the 19th century, the existence of the continent of Antarctica was considered by many people to be a myth.

Over the past century, through heroic exploration, humans have separated fact from legend—but the truth is often stranger than fiction. Islands "suddenly" appear in the sea. Fish that produce a sort of antifreeze in their blood swim beneath the ice of the Southern Ocean, while an active volcano, Mount Erebus, smolders above. In both the Arctic and Antarctic, a single "night" stretches on into weeks of bone-chilling cold and darkness.

The Arctic is mostly a sea world. At its heart is the Arctic Ocean, the world's smallest and shallowest ocean. This ocean is ringed by land, including parts of Europe, Asia, North America, and many islands. The Antarctic is mostly land—the continent of Antarctica—surrounded by ocean. The size and shape of the Arctic Ocean and the Antarctic continent are quite similar.

But there are great differences between these two icy worlds. More than 2 million people live within the Arctic Circle, while only a few thousand live in Antarctica. The largest Arctic animal is the polar bear. The largest permanent land-dweller of Antarctica is an insect about an eighth of an inch long!

Although they are half a world apart, both the Arctic and the Antarctic play an important role in life on Earth. Both, too, are fragile environments of danger and incredible beauty. This book will introduce you to some of the wonders of these frozen worlds.

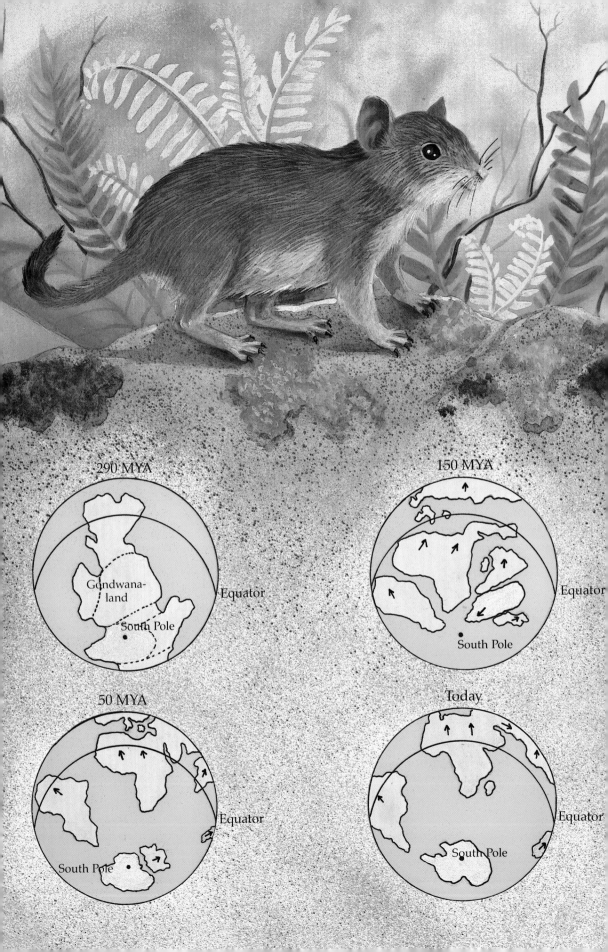

290 MYA

Gondwana-land

Equator

South Pole

150 MYA

Equator

South Pole

50 MYA

Equator

South Pole

Today

Equator

South Pole

Antarctica: Before the Ice

Nicknamed simply "The Ice," Antarctica is a land of extremes. This land, with its frigid blanket of ice and snow, has the highest average elevation of any continent—more than a mile above sea level. It's also the windiest place in the world. Winds of up to 50 miles per hour (mph) are common. Gusts of up to 200 mph are not unusual. Today, Antarctica is also the coldest place on Earth. The temperature seldom rises above freezing. At Vostok, a Russian research station, it once dipped to an astonishing −128°F!

Antarctica seems an unlikely land to have once supported trees and animals. However, exploration has turned up large coal seams (which are the remains of forests and swamps), and in 1981, the fossilized jaw of an ancient squirrel-sized mammal was discovered on a coastal island. Scientists concluded that, although Antarctica is now buried under two miles of ice, it was once ice-free and dotted with tropical forests! It was also much closer to Earth's equator.

Earth's continents are passengers on great crustal plates that, over millions of years, split and move about like bumper cars. This process is ongoing, but it happens very slowly. About 500 MYA (million years ago), Antarctica was part of a huge continent called Gondwanaland (gahn-DWAH-nuh-land), which also included Africa, India, South America, and Australia. At the time, sections of Antarctica straddled the equator. Then, about 180 MYA, giant Gondwanaland began to split apart. Inch by inch, Antarctica slowly crept to the bottom of the world. Its ice sheet began to form about 30 MYA. We can only guess about the creatures that once scampered through its forests or swam in its swamps. If any animal left its mark on the land, it is, at least for the time being, far beyond our reach beneath the ice.

Once covered with tropical forests, Antarctica has shifted to the bottom of the world and become the ice continent.

Ice Age Life

Over most of its history, the earth has been largely free of ice, and the climate has been generally warm. But every so often, the planet shivers through a cooling period known as an ice age. Ice ages occur millions of years apart. The most recent one, known simply as the Ice Age, began about 70,000 years ago and ended about 10,000 years ago. Ice sheets, in some places a mile thick, crept across much of northern Europe and North America. The land where New York City now stands was buried under millions of tons of ice. By the peak of the Ice Age, about 20,000 years ago, one-third of the planet was draped in a frigid cloak.

In some areas around the world the climate was pleasant. The Sahara, for example, now a vast, hot desert in Africa, was then a mild grassland. In places near the ice, however, the climate was extreme, especially in winter. Winds howled across cold, dry plains, raising great clouds of dust. Vegetation was sparse, but in some regions open forest provided winter food for animals. Summers were warm and sunny but very short.

Early humans lived in the shadow of great rivers of ice known as glaciers, but they prospered. Using a variety of tools, they hunted and killed large game, such as woolly mammoths, bison, and deer. With needles made of bone, they sewed the skins into protective clothing. They built shelters of animal bones covered with skins or sod.

Today we live in what might be called an ice-age intermission. The glaciers have retreated, but it is possible that they will return to cover the earth in a wintry blanket once again.

Early humans prospered in the shadow of Ice Age glaciers, depending mostly on animals for food, clothing, and shelter.

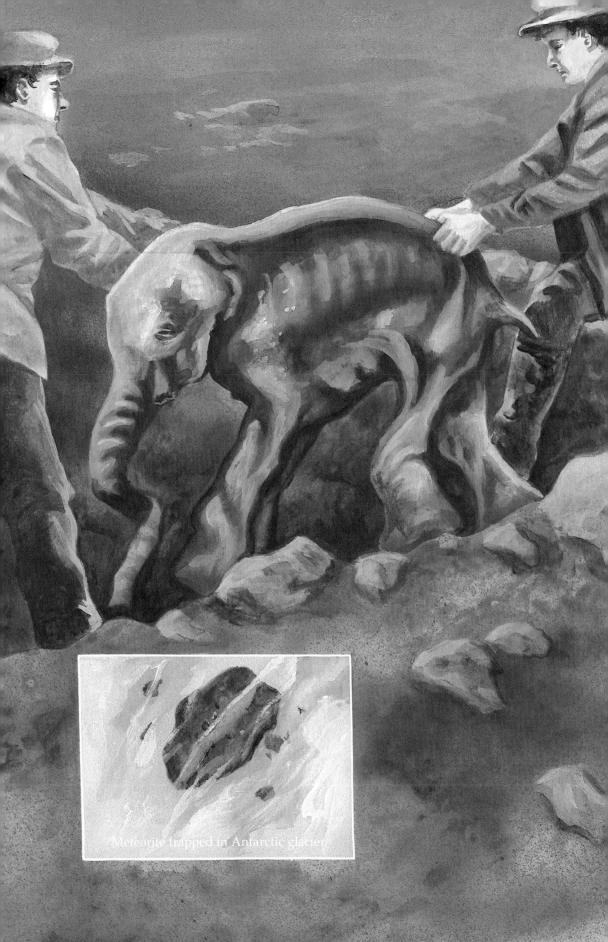

Meteorite trapped in Antarctic glacier

Frozen in Time

The surface of the Moon isn't the only place where moon rocks are found. Since 1982 scientists have discovered at least eight moon rocks trapped in Antarctic ice! How did they get there? Over millions of years, the Moon has been bombarded by asteroids and comets. Some collisions hurled rocks on the Moon's surface upward—so fast that they escaped the pull of lunar gravity. After journeys that averaged a million years, the fragments streaked through Earth's atmosphere between 70,000 and 170,000 years ago and tumbled to rest in the glaciers of Antarctica. There are other space rocks on Antarctica, too. Of the 6,000 meteorites that have been found there, most are bits from asteroids. However, a few may be from the planet Mars and some from even beyond our solar system. These rocks hold clues to the composition and history of our galaxy.

In the Arctic, it is the history not of the galaxy, but of the earth, that has emerged from the ice and frozen ground. For centuries of summer thaws in northern Siberia, the remains of huge, tusked animals have surfaced from the frozen soil. At first, people were not at all certain of what they were. Some thought they were the bones of giant humans. Others believed they were the remains of mammuts, ratlike beasts that weighed up to 10,000 pounds and reached lengths of nearly 20 feet. With its long tusks, a mammut supposedly burrowed underground because any exposure to air or sunlight was fatal. That explained why none had ever been found alive. Although natives found parts of hundreds of animals, it wasn't until 1806 that a whole carcass was brought to the Academy of Sciences in St. Petersburg. It then became clear that the remains, entombed thousands of years before, were not those of a giant human or rat, but those of the woolly mammoth.

Strange things have been found in northern lands,
like the whole carcass of an Ice Age woolly mammoth.

The World's Largest Ice Sheet

Nearly twice the size of Australia, Antarctica has no native human population. It's easy to see why. Ninety-eight percent of its land is, at this time, buried under a tremendous sheet of ice. The ice is so thick that if it were to spread out over the entire Earth, it would form a frosty layer 75 feet deep! More of the world's fresh water is locked into this southern sheet of ice than flows through all of our planet's rivers and lakes combined.

The massive ice sheet, and everything on it, is always slowly moving from inland areas of the continent to the sea. Thus, you could travel from the center of Antarctica to the coast without taking a step, although your trip would take thousands of years to complete! A number of speedy ice streams flow through the sheet like frigid currents. These ice streams, which are from 6 to 50 miles wide, rush seaward at rates of up to 1,600 feet a year. (That's from 10 to 100 times faster than the surrounding ice.) The "banks" of the streams, called chaos zones, are lined with jumbled piles of huge ice blocks. Scientists are still investigating the cause of these puzzling streams.

The ice sheet is also riddled with cracks called crevasses (cruh-VASS-uz). These cracks form as the ice moves over a rise or fall in the ground far below. The strain causes cracks in the brittle surface ice. The crevasses are sometimes as deep as 150 feet and wide enough to swallow a bulldozer. Often hidden under a flimsy bridge of snow, a crevasse can be very hazardous to travelers. When the sun shines, the dangerous gap may appear as a bluish shadow on the snow. However, when skies are overcast or when windswept snow is swirling in the air, a crevasse may be completely invisible.

The ice sheet of Antarctica is riddled with deep crevasses, which are sometimes covered by dangerously thin snow bridges.

Mummified seal

The Dry Valleys

When scientists first prepared to launch a space probe to Mars, they studied the problems they might face on that frigid desert planet by visiting the bizarre Dry Valleys of Antarctica. Nestled in the Transantarctic Mountains of Victoria Land, these strange, almost ice-free areas seem unearthly. Blue-white glaciers and towering ice cliffs drape the peaks that ring the valleys, filling the gaps between the peaks. The valley floors below are barren deserts of sand and rock: harsh winds that shriek down the mountain-sides quickly clear away any snow before it can build up.

Wright Valley is such a windswept oasis of land amid the icescape. It is easy to see that glaciers once moved across the basin because the valley has the "U" shape typically left behind by glaciers. Scarred boulders and the presence of frozen ground a few inches below the surface are further evidence of a glacial past.

In summer, Antarctica's largest meltwater river, the Onyx (ON-iks), runs through the Wright Valley to a small salt lake there known as Lake Vanda. The water at the bottom of this lake is 10 times saltier than seawater and can be as warm as 70°F. Why the salt levels are so high is a question that still baffles researchers. Lake Vanda has a thick, permanent cover of ice, but enough light penetrates the icy barrier for tiny blue-green algae to survive below.

The Dry Valleys hold another secret: preserved bodies of penguins and seals, some of them dead for several hundred years, have been found there. These animals are generally clumsy on land. How and why they ventured so far from the sea—only to die of starvation—is an unsolved mystery.

Mysteries of Antarctica's Dry Valleys include salty Lake Vanda and mummified penguins and seals.

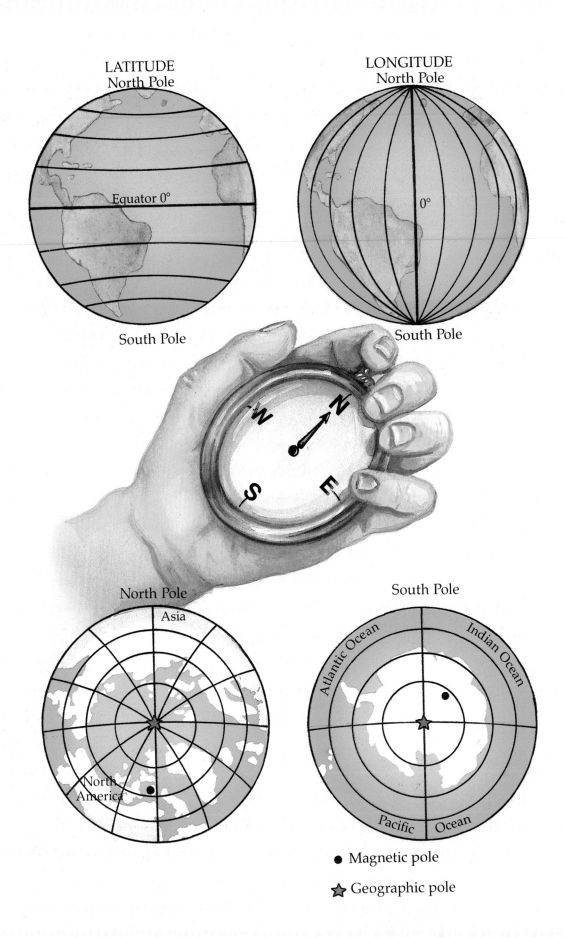

LATITUDE
North Pole

Equator 0°

South Pole

LONGITUDE
North Pole

0°

South Pole

North Pole

Asia

North
America

South Pole

Atlantic Ocean

Indian Ocean

Pacific Ocean

● Magnetic pole

★ Geographic pole

The Poles

The geographic poles are the most northerly and southerly points on Earth, and they are valuable reference points. To locate and describe any spot on the globe, navigators developed an imaginary grid. On this grid, horizontal lines, called parallels, ring the globe from the equator to each pole. These lines are used to describe distances, or "latitude," north or south of the equator. Imaginary vertical lines called meridians extend from pole to pole. These lines indicate distance, or "longitude," east and west of a line called the Prime Meridian that runs through Greenwich, England. Distances for both longitude and latitude are measured in units called degrees.

The magnetic poles are different from the geographic poles. The earth is surrounded by a magnetic field, just as a magnet is. The magnetic poles are the two points where this field comes in contact with the earth. A compass needle always points north—not to geographic north but to magnetic north. After taking a compass reading, navigators adjust their findings to *true* north (or geographic north) so they can determine their precise location.

The magnetic poles shift as much as a mile each year. Today the north magnetic pole is near Baffin Island, Canada. That is where a compass needle points. The south magnetic pole is just off the Adélie Coast, near Victoria Land. Scientists aren't certain what causes the magnetic poles to move. There is another mystery about the poles: Over the past 5 million years (and probably longer) they have reversed many times. This means that, from time to time, compass needles have pointed *south* instead of north! The baffling change occurs over several thousand years. The magnetic field grows slowly weaker until it seems to disappear, then it builds again in the opposite direction.

While the magnetic poles periodically shift, the geographic poles, based on lines of latitude and longitude, are stable.

Matt
Henson

Robert E.
Peary

Heroes of the Poles

The discovery of the North Pole is a story of great courage. On March 1, 1909, North Americans Robert E. Peary and Matt Henson headed north from Ellesmere Island in Canada with a small party. There was danger every step of the way. The ice buckled into huge ridges, or else split to reveal ribbons of icy water below. Storms whipped snow into the air, often making it impossible to see more than a few feet ahead. The intense cold threatened the explorers with frostbite, even death. Still, on April 6, Peary, Henson, and four Inuit guides reached the North Pole by dogsled, claiming it for all people.

The news disappointed a Norwegian explorer named Roald Amundsen, who had hoped to conquer the North Pole himself. Instead, he turned toward Antarctica. Robert F. Scott, an Englishman, had already planned a journey to the South Pole. Amundsen decided that he, too, would make the attempt. From different starting points, each set out in the summer of 1911. Glacier-covered mountains blocked the way inland, and conditions were just as difficult as those at the North Pole. After enduring terrible hardships, Scott and four companions reached the South Pole in January 1912, only to discover the Norwegian flag there. Amundsen had planted it on December 14, 1911. Bitterly disappointed, Scott's exhausted group began the long trek home, but they never arrived. Trapped by a storm, they died of cold and hunger only 11 miles from a supply of food.

Nine years later, in 1928, Amundsen vanished in the Arctic while searching for a missing friend. The two rivals, Scott and Amundsen, were thus entombed at opposite ends of the earth.

In hopes of conquering one of the poles, many explorers risked their lives.

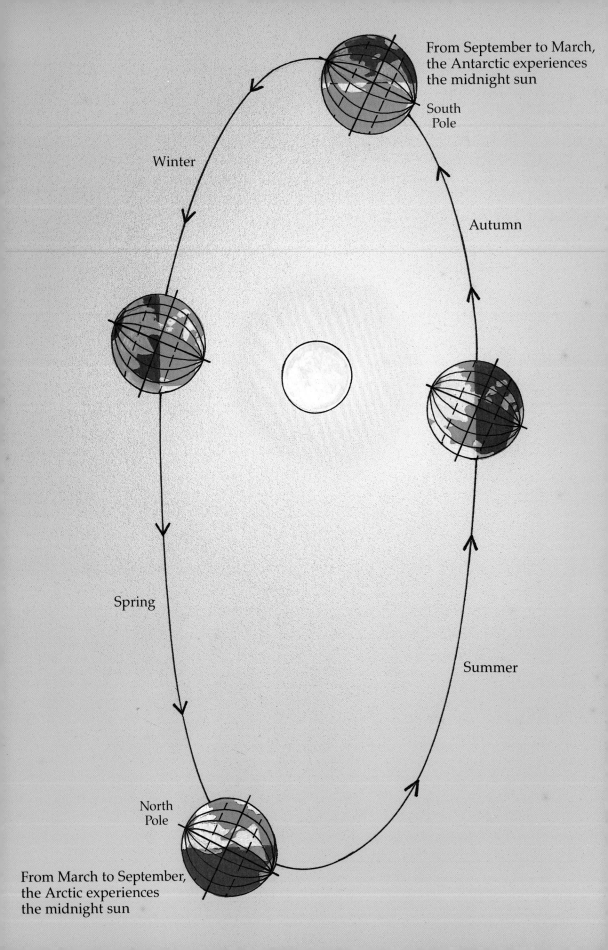

From September to March,
the Antarctic experiences
the midnight sun

South
Pole

Winter

Autumn

Spring

Summer

North
Pole

From March to September,
the Arctic experiences
the midnight sun

The Midnight Sun

Can you imagine reading a book by sunlight at midnight? It's possible to do this within the Arctic and Antarctic circles, where day and night are quite different from what we are used to. In these regions of the earth, there are several months of darkness in winter. The closer to one of the poles an area is, the longer it remains in complete darkness. In summer at the poles, the sun never sets below the horizon, so it is called "the midnight sun."

These unusually long days and nights occur because the earth is tilted slightly on its axis (an imaginary line that runs from pole to pole through the center of the planet). From March to September, Earth's northern hemisphere (its northern half) is tilted toward the sun. From September to March, the southern hemisphere is tilted toward the sun. Because of this tilt, each of the two polar regions is "shaded" from the sun by the rest of the planet for a large part of the year.

Spring arrives in Antarctica in September, when the sun first peeks above the horizon. Soon the sun rises high enough that it appears to circle slowly around the entire horizon, spiraling a little higher each day. After three months it reaches its highest position in the sky, then begins to spiral down again, finally sinking from view in March. The long, bitterly cold Antarctic "night" then begins. For several weeks, while the sun is just below the horizon, the continent is bathed in a ghostly twilight. The deepest darkness lasts for about three months. At the same time, the inhabitants of the Arctic Circle are enjoying the midnight sun.

Over a single year, each pole experiences both a period of constant light and a period of constant darkness.

Tierra del Fuego

Not all frigid southern lands lie within the Antarctic Circle. About 600 miles from Antarctica, at the tip of South America, there lies a scattering of islands known as Tierra del Fuego, which means "land of the fire." These islands could also be called "land of snow and rain" because the mountains in the west are capped with snow from April to November. In some areas, freezing rain pelts down for much of the year, helping the growth of Earth's most southerly rain forests.

How did this land get its name? North of the largest island, Isla Grande, there flows a wide, ice-free strait. In 1520, Ferdinand Magellan, a Portuguese navigator searching for a path from the Atlantic Ocean to the Pacific Ocean, turned his ships into this stormy channel. It took him 38 days to pass through. During that time, he noticed campfires burning to the south and dubbed the island Tierra del Fuego. The fires belonged to native Indians. Fine hunters, these hardy people fashioned harpoons, bows and arrows, slings, snares, and durable bark canoes. Some wore wraps or capes of fur, but many were so well adapted to the cold that they wore little in the way of clothing.

Among the animals that shared these lands with the Indians were huge, flightless birds called rheas, which were nearly six feet tall. The shores were crowded with herds of fur seals and scores of otters and penguins. Forests and grasslands were filled with guanacos, which are the largest land mammals in South America. This seven-foot-long relative of the camel provided the Indians with both food and fur.

After Magellan's journey, many more ships passed through the straits, bringing not only settlers, but also such diseases as measles and typhoid. Today, most of the animals are gone, and few, if any, Fuegan Indians survive.

Named for the campfires built by natives, Tierra del Fuego is a small cluster of islands at the tip of South America.

Fire and Ice

In the southeastern corner of Iceland there lies an ice cap called Vatnajokull (vat-nuh-YO-kul). It covers an area twice that of the Great Salt Lake of Utah and reaches depths of 3,000 feet. Beneath this huge slab of ice lies an unseen danger—a volcanic crater that holds a vast hidden lake. Every so often this active volcano erupts and causes a tremendous flood or "glacier burst." The waters of the hidden lake bubble over the volcano's edge and race down-hill under the ice for 30 miles. Spilling out onto a wide plain, the warm water fans out into a shallow, sulphur-scented pool that stretches for many miles.

Such strange activity is not unusual in Iceland. This island country has more hot springs and vents than any other area of the world. Smaller than Wyoming, Iceland is crowded with some 200 volcanoes. Nearly one-third of the world's surface lava formations shaped over the last 500 years are here. Icy glaciers blanket 10 percent of this unusual land of the far north. This island is actually the top of a great volcano that is just one of many active vol-canoes joined together. They form a chain that rises from the middle of the ocean floor and stretches the entire length of the Atlantic Ocean.

A remarkable example of the sea-floor activity in this area was the creation of Surtsey (SERT-see) Island off the southern coast of Iceland. This amazing event first came to human attention on November 14, 1963, when the night watch on a fishing vessel spied what was thought to be a burning ship on the horizon. The following afternoon, waves were seen breaking on something just below the surface. By evening, amid smoke and fire, Surtsey's volcanic tip peeked above the frigid sea, and an island was born.

Many islands have been created by exploding volcanoes, like Iceland's Surtsey Island.

Mount Kilimanjaro

Glaciers at the Equator

Glacial ice is found on every continent except Australia. In East Africa, glaciers that formed during the Ice Age still glisten within 200 miles of the sun-drenched equator. They crown the peaks of ancient volcanoes such as Mount Kilimanjaro (kil-uh-mun-JAR-o).

Kibo, the central cone of Mount Kilimanjaro, soars more than 19,000 feet into the air. About one and a half square miles of ice coat its upper slopes. Surprisingly, when the ice first formed, the climate of Africa was not much cooler than it is today. Atop Kilimanjaro, however, the air was, and still is, much colder. (Air absorbs much of the warmth that is radiated from the earth and some warmth from the sun. As you go higher, the atmosphere is thinner and absorbs less heat, so the air is colder.) It is here, atop Kilimanjaro, where the glaciers were born thousands of years ago. In winter, snow fell among the craggy peaks. Gathering into heavy piles, particularly on the shaded side of the mountain, much of it lasted through the summer. Each year the amount of permanent snow increased, blanketing the summit in white. Over centuries, the weight of the upper layers of snow compressed those at the bottom into solid ice. Finally, under the pressure of their own weight and the pull of gravity, the young glaciers began to slip down the mountain slopes.

The frozen rivers crept to within a mile or two of the African plain, but as the Ice Age ended the climate warmed and the glaciers began to shrink. By the 19th century, the lower peaks of Kilimanjaro were clear of ice. Today, the glaciers dip no lower than 15,000 feet high on the mountainside, and streams of meltwater gouge deep channels in the ice. Unless the earth's climate cools once more, the glaciers of equatorial Africa will be gone by the end of this century.

Deep channels in glaciers, like those on Mount Kilimanjaro, were caused by streams of meltwater after the Ice Age.

Avalanches and Blizzards

In the Arctic, the warmest place to be is usually deep in the snow! Many Arctic creatures burrow into it for protection from the cold and wind. Air trapped in the snow serves as insulation and helps to keep the animals warm. Soil that lies beneath a blanket of snow is also warmer than the air above. The snow nearest the ground may even melt a little and become grainy, like sugar. This type of snow is unstable and dangerous if it lies on a slope. As snow builds up, the grainy layer can slip, sending a wave of ice and snow roaring down the mountain. This wave, known as an avalanche, may reach speeds of 200 mph. Strong winds rushing ahead of the wave can topple trees. Also called the white death, avalanches kill about 150 people a year.

In 1962, a small town in Peru suffered the fury of an avalanche that was the worst of its kind in history. The townspeople were settling down to their evening meal when a strange rumbling echoed through the valley. Above in the mountains, a huge section of a glacier had slipped. About 20 million tons of mud, rocks, ice, and snow rocketed toward the village. Minutes later, the terrible avalanche had buried more than 4,000 people in a tomb 10 miles long and 60 feet deep.

Another icy danger is the blizzard. Driven by winds of at least 35 mph, these snowstorms may cause accidents or trap people in their homes. The worst blizzard in the history of New York City struck without warning on March 12, 1888. Light snow fell in the morning, but by the afternoon winds of up to 100 mph were lashing the city, tearing up trees, and piling snow in drifts up to 15 feet high. When the blizzard had passed, 200 people were dead. The vicious storm then thrashed its way along the East Coast, claiming another 600 lives before it waned.

Claiming the lives of more than 4,000 people, an avalanche weighing almost 20 million tons struck a small town in Peru.

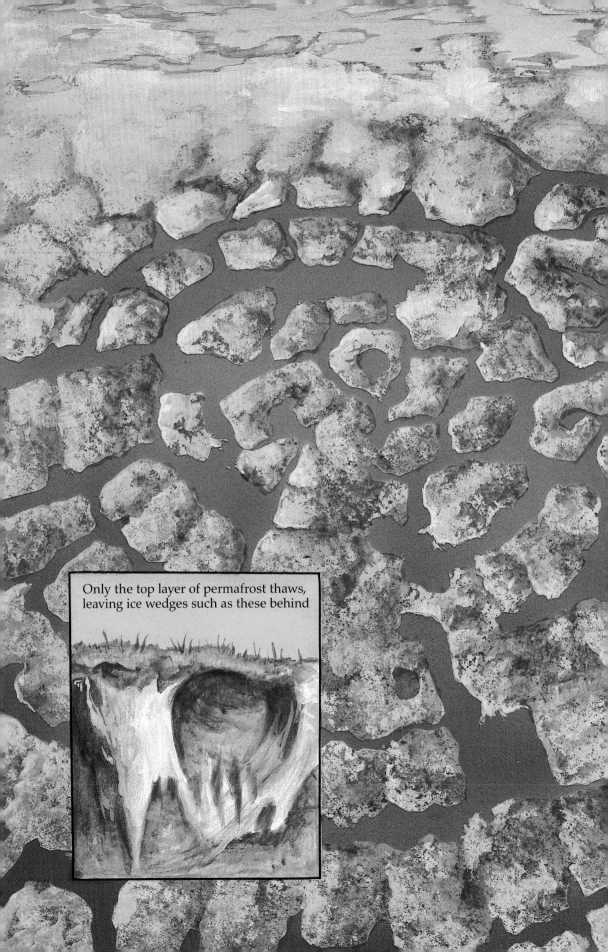

Only the top layer of permafrost thaws, leaving ice wedges such as these behind

Permafrost

From scorching deserts and muggy jungles, to stormy shorelines and grass-covered plains, there are many environments on Earth. The youngest of Earth's environments is the Arctic tundra—treeless plains that developed as the glaciers of the Ice Age retreated. In winter much of the tundra is covered by snow and ice. Even in sunny summer the ice is near, just a few inches beneath the surface in the permanently frozen ground called permafrost. Made of sand, gravel, or clay, permafrost may be dry (such as in the Dry Valleys of Antarctica) or icy (as in the Arctic tundra). Permafrost lies beneath one-quarter of the earth's land surface, including most of Alaska and half of both Canada and the Soviet Union. In some places it has existed for thousands of years and may be 1,500 feet deep or more.

Permafrost prevents moisture in the soil from draining away, but it also prevents the growth of plants with deep root systems, such as tall trees. The roots of Arctic plants are generally in the top few inches of soil, known as the active layer. This layer is seldom more than three feet deep and thaws in summer, making water available to plants and animals. The sodden summer soil can be a problem, though. Loose and muddy, it may creep downslope, burying some plants and carrying others to less desirable spots.

Permafrost poses an interesting problem for humans, too. In spring, buildings can sink or tilt in the thawed soil. Even in winter, heat from a building can pass through the floor and thaw the permafrost below. Because of this, some homes are built on short stilts or on mounds of gravel that allow cold air to circulate beneath the floor.

Because of the constant freezing and thawing of the permafrost, strange patterns in the topsoil layer result.

Plant Strategies

In the grip of winter, the Arctic tundra is generally covered with a blanket of ice and snow. By spring, however, the ground beneath the snow begins to stir, and by summer it is bursting with life. About 400 different kinds of plants have adapted to the demanding Arctic climate by developing ways to cope with the cold, the wind, and the very brief growing season.

Many Arctic plants grow from underground parts, such as bulbs, corms, and rhizomes (RY-zomz). These parts allow the plants to store nutrients below the surface. After sprouting from these "storage units" in spring, the plants rarely grow more than a few inches tall, and most hug the ground. This protects them from the dry winds that howl across the open plains, even in summer. Life-giving summer sunshine lasts for only a few weeks, so Arctic plants sprout, bloom, produce seeds, and wither very rapidly. The colorful purple mountain saxifrage (SAKS-ih-fraj) can blossom and produce seeds in less than a month. A head start always helps, too: Arctic cotton grass can grow sooner than its neighbors. Because this plant grows in a tight clump, it shields and warms the ground beneath it. The warmed soil expands and actually lifts the snow-covered plant upward, enabling it to catch more of the sun's rays. The snow on the plant melts away several days sooner than that of its neighbors.

Other Arctic plants use different methods to stay warm. The flower of the buttercup moves to follow the path of the sun. The flower's shape also channels solar warmth toward the developing seeds at its center. Fuzzy coats of fibers insulate the stems and buds of many plants, such as the woolly lousewort, from the cold. Other plants grow in tight clusters that conserve heat. The temperature within a dense, leafy tuft of saxifrage may be 10 degrees warmer than that of the surrounding air.

Adapted for survival through the harsh winter, hundreds of Arctic plants thrive in the thaw of spring.

Arctic bumblebee

Blackfly

Arctic butterfly

Warble fly larva

Warble fly

Arctic Insects

You won't find grasshoppers or ants in the Arctic, but the land of the midnight sun is not without insects. Although few species are native to the area, in the warm season millions of flies, mosquitoes, bees, beetles, and butterflies spread across the land. The last three arrive just in the nick of time to pollinate the tundra plants during the short growing season. And one type of Arctic orchid is pollinated by a nectar-eating mosquito! The buzzing, creeping, and crawling multitudes also provide a critical source of food for Arctic birds and other animals.

The insect legions, however, often cause suffering to some tundra residents. Blood-sucking flies and mosquitoes may attack in such tremendous numbers that they can drain the life from small, warm-blooded prey. Caribou are the unwilling targets of the warble fly. The female fly lays her eggs on the caribou's legs, and within days newly hatched larvae burrow under the animal's skin to its back. They grow to nearly an inch long before tunneling out through the hide.

Arctic insects have adjusted to the constant cold, just as the plants have. They are generally darker (dark colors absorb more of the sun's warmth), smaller, and "fuzzier" than similar warm-weather insects. Those that fly stay close to the ground where the air is warmest. By vibrating their wings, Arctic bees produce heat to keep the insides of their nests much warmer than the outside air. Most insects avoid the Arctic winter altogether. As the summer days grow short, some take shelter under rocks or in the soil. The eggs or larvae of many insects actually spend the winter frozen into ponds or bogs. In spring, one square yard of thawed fresh water in the tundra can produce up to 100,000 insects!

While some Arctic insects have adjusted to the constant cold, most take shelter each winter under rocks or in soil.

Lapps scraping reindeer skins

People of Frozen Lands

Although the climate is harsh, many people make their homes in the Arctic. The word _Eskimo,_ a Cree Indian word that means "eaters of raw meat," is often used to describe the hardy natives of the American North. These natives call themselves Inuit (IN-oo-it), which means, simply, "the people."

Because of the brief growing season, farming is not practical on the tundra. The Inuit rely instead on hunting to satisfy many of their needs. For centuries, the early inland dwellers hunted caribou. Coastal residents hunted walrus, seals, and whales. No part of an animal was wasted. The meat was eaten lightly boiled, frozen, or dried. The fat was burned as fuel in stone lamps. The Inuit carved the bones into tools and stretched the skins to serve as waterproof coverings for shelters or boats. For protection from the cold, the Inuit fashioned furs into warm clothing. Today, modern conveniences make life more comfortable for the Inuit, but the traditional ways have not been completely discarded.

Across the Arctic Sea lives another hearty race, the Lapps. Lapland is not a country but a region that lies in northern Scandinavia and the Soviet Union. Like the Inuit, the Lapps depend on animals for their sustenance, but instead of hunting them, they actually raise and care for their herds of reindeer (the Eurasian name for caribou). Until the mid-20th century, reindeer provided the Lapps with everything they needed—meat and milk for food and warm skins for clothing and shelter. In fact, the Lapp word for a reindeer herd means "what one lives on." When the herds migrated, many Lapp families moved with them, living in cone-shaped tents that looked much like American Indian tepees. The modern age, however, is bringing many changes to the Lapps' way of life. Few families continue to follow the herds, and many young Lapps have chosen a more modern lifestyle in the city.

The Inuits and Lapps live on the harsh tundra, where they depend on animals, like reindeer and fish, for food and clothing.

First row of snow blocks

More blocks are added

Final block is cut to fit top
of dome

Finished igloo with cutaway
to show beds

Entrance through tunnel

The Igloo

Can you imagine living in a home made entirely of ice and snow? The igloo, which is most commonly built by the Canadian Inuit, is just such a place. Igloos are not permanent homes but winter shelters that are used during travel or on hunting expeditions. A practiced builder can make one in an hour, using blocks of hard packed snow called upsik. With a special saw up to 20 inches long, the builder slices the upsik into large blocks that are about 4 feet long, 2 feet wide, and 8 inches thick. These blocks form the igloo's foundation, which is usually about 10 feet in diameter. The blocks that follow are all cut at an angle, so that each new layer will lean further in toward the center and give the igloo a dome shape. When the structure is around 9 feet high, the builder cuts a final block and fits it into position. This last block holds everything securely in place.

Next, it is time for the finishing touches. If the ground is soft enough, the builder digs an entry tunnel under the foundation. Often, however, the ground is frozen solid, so the occupant cuts a door into the igloo and constructs an above-ground snow-block entry tunnel (usually about 10 feet long). A skin may be hung across the entryway to keep out any drafts. Trapped body warmth and perhaps an oil lamp heat the igloo inside. Excess heat and smoke escape through a tiny opening carved in the roof. If a slab of clear sea ice can be found, the igloo can even be given a window.

To furnish the igloo, the builder forms a sleeping platform from snow. Covered with willow branches and thick furs, the platform is warm and snug. Even with a raging storm howling outside, a traveler can survive very cozily for many days in a well-made igloo.

Used only for temporary shelter, an igloo is made entirely of the Arctic's most plentiful elements: snow and ice.

This Weddell seal has cut a
breathing hole through the ice.

Seals of North and South

Inland, the continent of Antarctica is almost lifeless. The coastline and surrounding sea, however, are home to many creatures. One of these is the 9-foot-long, 500-pound crabeater seal, which is the most abundant seal in the world. Millions of these seals live on the Antarctic Ocean on rafts of pack ice. The crabeater seal's main food is not crab, as its name suggests, but a shrimplike animal known as krill. The seal's cheek teeth are designed to filter the krill from the water. Unlike most seals, the crabeater is agile out of water and can clamber over the ice at speeds of up to 15 mph.

The Weddell (WED-ul) seal is about the same length, but at around 950 pounds it is chubbier than the crabeater. It also lives farther south on the coast and on fast ice (ice that is securely attached to land). It spends a great deal of its time streaking through the frigid waters, searching for fish and squid to eat. This seal even hunts under the ice, catching breaths of air through small holes that it carves with its strong canine teeth. It can dive to 2,000 feet deep and remain underwater for up to 45 minutes.

The Antarctic is also home to the only seal that regularly eats warm-blooded prey . . . the leopard seal. Named for its spotted coat, this seal is a graceful swimmer and cunning hunter. It swims near the edge of the ice, waiting for its prey—penguins or young Weddell seals—to enter the water.

In the Arctic, the most common seal is the ringed seal. The smallest of the true seals at 5 feet long and less than 200 pounds, it also lives farthest north. It winters in the water, under sheets of fast ice. Using the sharp, heavy nails on its front flippers, it carves small breathing holes called aglus (AG-looz) in the ice. It also carves holes large enough for hauling itself out of the water.

This ringed seal and its pup live in the far north. Some seals, like the Weddell seal, make their home in southern waters.

Crocodile fish

Ice fish

Octopus

Sea spider

Greenland shark

Coral

Life in the Frigid Seas

At both poles, the icy waters teem with life. The most abundant creatures are krill. There can be up to 35 pounds of krill in an area about the size of a bathtub. Only 1 or 2 inches long, these animals feed on tiny ocean plants called phytoplankton. The krill themselves are food for other creatures, including the blue whale, the largest living animal in the world. This 100-foot-long whale eats several tons of krill each day.

The darkened sea floor harbors dozens of other kinds of sea dwellers, such as brightly colored anemones (uh-NEM-o-neez), sea snails, sponges, wolf eels, giant barnacles, and starfish. One bizarre resident of the Antarctic sea bottom is the giant sea spider. This slow-moving animal stretches 10 inches from the tip of one long, slender leg to another, but it has a very tiny head and body. In fact, the sea spider's body is so small that most of the creature's internal organs are in its spindly legs!

One of the sea spider's neighbors is the scaleless, almost transparent ice fish. The largest of these fish are 2 feet long and weigh 5 pounds. This ghostly fish has no red blood cells and no hemoglobin (the substance in blood that carries oxygen). The pale blood is not very efficient for delivering oxygen, but the ice fish makes up for quality with quantity: it has up to four times as much blood as a similar-sized, warm-water fish.

Sharks are rare in polar waters, with one exception—the Arctic Greenland shark, which can reach lengths of up to 14 feet. This shark is also called the sleeper shark because of its sluggish nature. The meat of the Greenland shark is edible by humans if prepared carefully. If not, it can cause an illness in which the victim appears very drunk. In fact, the Inuit refer to someone who has had too much alcohol to drink as "shark-sick."

The icy waters around the North and South poles teem with amazing sea life found only in these remote areas.

The Adélie Penguin

Along with its neighbor, the emperor penguin, the Adélie (uh-DAY-lee) penguin can survive in colder weather than can any other animal. Like most penguins, the Adélie (named for the wife of a homesick French explorer) spends most of its time at sea. A thick layer of blubber under its skin keeps this bird warm even in the icy waters, and a cozy covering of closely packed, waterproof feathers keeps it dry.

Although it cannot fly, the Adélie is a great swimmer. Powered by paddlelike wings, it swims at a speed of about 15 mph—four times faster than that of a human. This penguin has a special way of leaving the water. It first dives deep, then turns toward the surface and races upward. Picking up speed, it shoots above the surface and pops out onto the shore like a cork.

An adult penguin builds its nest on land, where it has no natural predators. In spring, the Adélie treks inland across fields of frozen sea ice to reach its breeding ground, or rookery, on the coast. Here, the melting snow exposes the pebbly land beneath. Pebbles are the building material for the Adélie's nest, and they are used by males as gifts for potential mates. Because thousands of birds gather in the same area to build their nests, pebbles are soon in short supply. A male usually steals a suitable one from another bird's nest to present it to a female as a gift. If the female accepts it, the pair sing noisily to each other. While they are occupied, another male may steal the same pebble!

The birds must lay their eggs and raise their young in three or four months, before the short polar day ends. It is a race for survival. At two months old, the young are almost fully developed. As the long night approaches once again, all of the penguins head for the sea.

Adélie penguins build their nests each spring with pebbles found along the Antarctic coast.

The Polar Bear

The polar bear is the most powerful land predator in the Arctic. One of the world's largest bears, it grows to 8 feet long and more than 5 feet high at the shoulder. Some polar bears weigh as much as 1,500 pounds. This massive animal is an expert hunter. It preys mainly upon seals, feasting only on the blubber. With its fine sense of smell, it can locate and track a seal more than 20 miles away. It can also discover and open seal dens that are hidden 3 feet deep below the snow and ice. If the bear cannot find a seal, however, it will make do with whatever is available— including walrus, fish, and even kelp (a large, leafy sea plant).

Like all polar animals, this bear has developed special adaptations to help it to survive in its icy habitat. Long hair that grows from between the animal's claw-tipped toes provides better footing on the slippery ice. A thick layer of blubber under the polar bear's skin helps it to remain comfortable in weather well below freezing. Its luxurious coat is made up of two types of hair. Long, outer guard hairs shed water easily to keep the animal dry. The shorter, woolly hairs of its undercoat protect it from the biting cold. This coat helps to keep the polar bear warm in another way, too. Although the hair appears white, it is actually clear and hollow. Serving somewhat like light traps, the hollow hairs collect ultraviolet light from the sun, convert it to heat, and carry it toward the animal's skin. Under its snow-colored coat, the bear's charcoal black skin absorbs the heat. Surprisingly, this process only works in one direction, so little of the bear's body heat is lost to the environment.

The polar bear, regarded as the most powerful land predator in the Arctic, teaches its young how to hunt.

The Musk Ox

The musk ox is well equipped to withstand the harsh conditions of its wintry world. The largest of all grazing animals on the Arctic tundra, this eight-foot-long creature is covered with long, dense hair that reaches almost to its feet. Feeding on mosses and other plants in spring and summer, the musk ox builds up fat reserves that also help to protect it from winter's chill.

These animals band together in herds of 10 or 15, led by a male (or bull). During the mating season (from midsummer to fall), the herds gather into much larger groups. Then the bulls clash in furious duels over females. The bulls emit a strong, musky odor from glands on their faces. A challenge between two males begins when one scrapes a small hole in the dirt, then kneels on its forelegs to rub its scent glands around the hole. The males then approach each other in a cautious, sideways prance, bellowing all the while. One or the other finally breaks the standoff by charging at its rival with its head lowered, brandishing its curved horns, which can be up to two feet long.

The musk ox thrived during the Ice Age. With the close of that period, however, it had to survive the gradual warming of the climate. As its range narrowed to just the tundra of North America, the musk ox faced an even greater peril: humans. Over time, these other Ice Age survivors have hunted the oxen nearly to extinction. When a herd of musk oxen is threatened, perhaps by wolves, the adults form a protective circle around the calves. Lowering their horns, they stand their ground. But this strategy worked poorly against armed humans who hunted them for their fur. Eventually, people realized that because the musk ox sheds its plush underfur in thick sheets, these could be gathered and knit into soft wool with no harm to the animal at all. Now, the future of the musk ox is brighter, and herds in Canada and Greenland are increasing.

One of the few survivors of the Ice Age, musk oxen once roamed with now-extinct woolly rhinos and mammoths.

Beluga whale

The Killer Whale and the Beluga

Despite its name, the killer whale is actually the largest member of the dolphin family. Up to 30 feet long and weighing as much as 9 tons, it is the only dolphin known to feed on warm-blooded animals. While it roves most of the earth's oceans, it prefers cold polar waters, both north and south. Equipped with about 40 sharp teeth for biting and holding its prey, the killer whale is a fearsome hunter. It feeds on a wide variety of animals, including penguins, walrus pups, sharks, and squid, and it can swallow a seal whole. Also called the "wolf of the sea," the killer whale has an excellent sense of smell, which it probably uses to help locate its meals. Able to reach speeds of 35 mph, it stands a good chance of catching what it finds. The killer whale is among the most intelligent of sea mammals, and entire family groups (or pods) may cooperate in the hunt. They rarely bother humans, but killer whales will attack other dolphins and whales, including the Arctic beluga whale.

In Russian, *beluga* means "white," and there is no doubt how this animal got its name. Although the beluga whale is a dark blue-gray color when it is born, it soon turns snowy white. The beluga is also called the "sea canary" because it makes a wide range of sounds. By altering the shape of a large bulge, called a melon, at the front of its head, it controls and directs the sounds it makes. Beluga whales tour Arctic coastal waters in small groups, feeding on fish and crustaceans. Often, they swim far into open channels in the ice pack, or even into rivers. Polar bears and humans prey upon this slow-moving animal, but the predator the beluga seems to fear most is the killer whale. Salmon fishermen in Alaska use this fear to protect their catch: they broadcast underwater recordings of killer whale calls to scare off hungry belugas.

The fearless killer whale will swim extremely close to shore to catch its prey, which includes seals and beluga whales.

Reindeer and Caribou

If you looked at pictures of a Eurasian reindeer and of a North American caribou and thought that these animals seemed identical, you'd be right. Since the 1950s, scientists have considered these six-foot-long, four-foot-tall members of the deer family to be the same species.

In summer, these majestic animals of the tundra have coats of dark fur with collars of snowy white. As winter approaches, long, pale, hollow hairs called guard hairs grow in to act as insulation. Even the animal's nose is fur-covered! Unlike most other deer, both male and female caribou and reindeer sport magnificent antlers. Those of the male may spread four feet across. Each year the animals shed their antlers and grow a new pair covered with tender skin known as velvet. By late summer, the velvet is shed and each animal's stately crown is complete.

Grazing animals, both reindeer and caribou feed on a variety of plants. When winter's snow hides the ground, they scrape the frosty covering away to find food such as reindeer moss. Large herds, often numbering in the thousands, migrate each year in search of food. Some migration routes cover distances of hundreds of miles and have been in use for centuries. Although hunted by humans, the caribou of North America are wild and travel freely. Reindeer herds are closely supervised by the Lapps of Eurasia. Each spring, Lapp herders drive the animals to small islands or into the mountains to graze. In fall, the herders round the reindeer up into enclosures. At that time they choose some animals to send to market and they notch the ears of newborn calves so that they can be identified the following year.

Reindeer and caribou shed the velvet from their huge antlers in late summer.

The March of the Lemmings

The Norway lemming has lived in Scandinavia since the Ice Age. This little rodent is only six inches long and weighs just three ounces, but it is remarkable in a number of ways. It lives hidden in the coarse grass in the summertime, and in winter it digs tunnels beneath the snow and makes a nest of twigs, grass, and fur. The lemming feeds on grass, moss, and lichens.

When food is plentiful, another of this lemming's amazing traits becomes apparent. It can reproduce at an astounding rate. A newborn female lemming is ready to breed within three weeks of birth, and she can deliver her own litter just three weeks later. There are between five and eleven babies in each litter, and females may have as many as five litters every year. Under perfect conditions, a pair of lemmings and their offspring could build a population of about 170 million animals in just one year! Conditions are seldom perfect, of course, and lemmings also have many enemies, such as foxes, stoats, and owls. Scientists once observed an owl capture 83 lemmings in one week to feed its chicks.

About once every four years, when the Norway lemming populations are at their peak, thousands of these animals begin a strange migration. Striking out in search of food, the tiny creatures cover distances of nearly three miles a day. Faced with a barrier such as a stream, they try to swim across. If the watery obstacle is a wide river or even the sea, many lemmings lose their lives in the attempt to cross. This has given rise to a legend that they sacrifice themselves so that there will be plenty of food for those left behind. Although the lemming is a brave and hardy creature, this is not the case. Indeed, though many die during the migration, others survive to find new feeding grounds.

Once every four years, thousands of Norway lemmings migrate in search of food, often crossing rivers or seas.

The Fox and the Hare

Only one Arctic animal appears to seek out the company of the powerful polar bear, and that is the little Arctic fox. About two feet long, not counting its luxurious tail, this fox takes advantage of the bear's skill as a hunter and hangs around to clean up any scraps. The fox will also eat anything it can find itself, including rodents, eggs, berries, and even garbage. It often stores food for the winter in rocky crevices.

Active all year long, the Arctic fox may take shelter from harsh winter weather by burrowing into riverbanks and snowbanks. It is, however, well prepared for the cold. With its thick, soft coat of warm fur, it can withstand temperatures as low as −100°F! In winter its fur is generally white. In summer the Arctic fox has two color phases: during one phase its fur is a creamy color with dark tips, and during the other it is a grayish-blue. Some foxes exhibit both summer phases, but most show one or the other. This fox is the only member of the dog family to change color.

Among the prey of the Arctic fox is the world's most northerly hare, the Arctic hare. At the southern edge of its range, this hare also changes color with the seasons, showing a soft, rich brown in summer and a milky white in winter. At the northern edge of its range, the hare keeps its white coat all year. In summer, the Arctic hare usually feeds alone on the sparse vegetation. In autumn, the hares form large herds. There are few hiding places on the tundra for either prey or predator. By standing up on its hind feet, the Arctic hare can easily keep watch on its surroundings, and it can even run in a standing position. The fact that entire groups will sometimes flee in this manner encouraged a charming old tale that Arctic hares often pass the time by dancing together.

The Arctic fox eats anything it can find for itself, including the Arctic hare.

Dall's sheep

Mountain Dwellers

The Himalayas, the magnificent mountains of Central Asia, are home to one of the rarest and most beautiful of the great cats—the snow leopard. Also known as the ounce, in summer this animal wanders as high as 19,000 feet up toward the peaks. In winter it seeks milder weather, going as far as 6,500 feet down the mountainside. This big cat is protected from the cold of its wintry habitat by a thick coat of soft, pale fur, which has dark spots. The hair between the leopard's footpads grows very long, so that even the soles of its feet are cushioned by soft fur.

This cat preys upon deer, wild sheep, rodents, and birds. It relies on surprise to capture its prey, cautiously stalking its victim and then pouncing. A skilled hunter, the snow leopard is credited with amazing leaps of 50 feet or more. It is capable of brief bursts of speed, but it seldom gives chase for long. If the big cat cannot catch its meal within a short distance, it conserves its energy and waits for a better opportunity.

Another surefooted mountain dweller is the Dall's sheep of the snow-capped mountains of North America. These 5-foot-long, 200-pound animals rove in small bands high among the craggy peaks of Alaska and northwestern Canada, grazing on grasses and lichens. Large hooves with hard rims and soft centers give this master climber a good grip, even across the icy face of a steep cliff. In the southern part of its range, this sheep may be almost black. In the north, its thick coat is snowy white. Both male and female Dall's sheep have wide, gently curving horns. In autumn, males use their horns in mating clashes. Charging head on, they crash together with a resounding CRACK that can be heard for miles. The stronger male wins his mate, while the loser must settle for a headache.

Two mountain dwellers: the meat-eating snow leopard of Asia and the grass-eating Dall's sheep of North America.

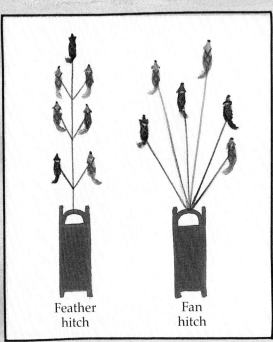

Feather
hitch

Fan
hitch

Dogs of the Ice

The successful exploration of Earth's polar regions would certainly have been more difficult without the hardy sled dog. Although not native to the poles, these brave animals have drawn sleds over endless fields of ice and snow. Encouraged by the command "hut hut hut," teams of dogs have been used to deliver mail, food, and medical supplies. They have accompanied humans to some of the most remote and hostile areas of the earth. Robert Peary said of his dog teams that they had carried his band of explorers "where no other power on earth could have moved them."

An experienced dog team can continue at a steady pace for 18 hours straight, and, over level ground, the team can reach speeds of up to 20 mph. A popular annual contest of sled-dog ability is the Alaskan Iditarod (eye-DIT-uh-rod) dogsled race from Anchorage to Nome. The grueling course covers 1,200 miles of rugged territory that severely tests a team and its handler.

Many people call all sled dogs "huskies," but actually a number of different breeds make excellent sled dogs— for example, the strong, intelligent Greenland husky, the good-natured Siberian husky, the sure-footed Alaskan malamute, and the sturdy Samoyed. Most are descended from wolves. But whatever the breed, sled dogs have certain things in common. With fairly short, extremely thick fur, they are comfortable in temperatures as low as −30°F. While on a journey, these dogs sleep out in the open, usually covered by an insulating blanket of snow. They thrive on frozen meat and fish. Strong, stalwart, and loyal, good sled dogs also have plenty of stamina and courage, something their handlers call "heart."

Teams of sled dogs, either in feather-hitch or fan-hitch formation, are used to carry supplies for parties of explorers.

Ice Worlds

Earth's frozen worlds may seem quite distant, but they affect us all in many ways. The poles actually act as a sort of planetary air conditioner. The earth absorbs much more heat from the sun than it reflects. If it absorbed all the heat it received, our world could grow too warm to sustain life. Fortunately, the ice at the poles reflects more of the sun's heat than it absorbs. Also, cold polar ocean currents that flow toward the equator help to regulate the climate of the entire planet. Even polar plant life is involved in climate control. Phytoplankton, the tiny sea plants that fill polar waters during the springtime, absorb carbon dioxide. (This gas, when it collects to high levels in the air, contributes to a dangerous warming of the earth's atmosphere known as the greenhouse effect.) The poles are also home to many remarkable animals. Dozens of species of birds, whales, seals, and fish feed on the krill that thrive in the frigid waters.

But our ice worlds are fragile and need protection. Unfortunately, both polar seas have already been stained by oil spills. Entire populations of Arctic animals teeter on the verge of extinction as their habitats are altered. Hunted by humans over the past 200 years, less than 10 percent of the Antarctic whale population survives. Without proper monitoring, both northern and southern oceans could easily be overfished. Perhaps even more serious, possible mineral wealth hidden under the ice could lead to the development and misuse of Antarctica. However, if nations of the world cooperate with one another, we can correct or avoid these misuses of our polar environments. This is a responsibility we must all take seriously, because our remote, sometimes hostile, often beautiful polar worlds are critical to the survival of our planet.

For Further Reading

De Quetteville, Gordon: *Glaciers and Ice Sheets,* New York City, The Bookwright Press, 1984.

Fradin, Dennis Brindell: *Disaster! Blizzards,* Chicago, Children's Press, 1983.

Gallant, Roy A.: *The Ice Ages,* New York City, Franklin Watts, 1985.

Nixon, Hershell H., and Nixon, Joan Lowery: *Glaciers,* New York City, Dodd, Mead & Co., 1980.

Sandak, Cass R.: *The Arctic and Antarctic,* New York City, Franklin Watts, 1987.

Sharp, David: *Animal Days: Animals from Cold Lands,* Kensington, Australia, Bay Books, 1984.

Williams, Terry Tempest, and Major, Ted: *The Secret Language of Snow,* San Francisco, Sierra Club Books, 1984.

Index